THINGS
THAT
MEASURE

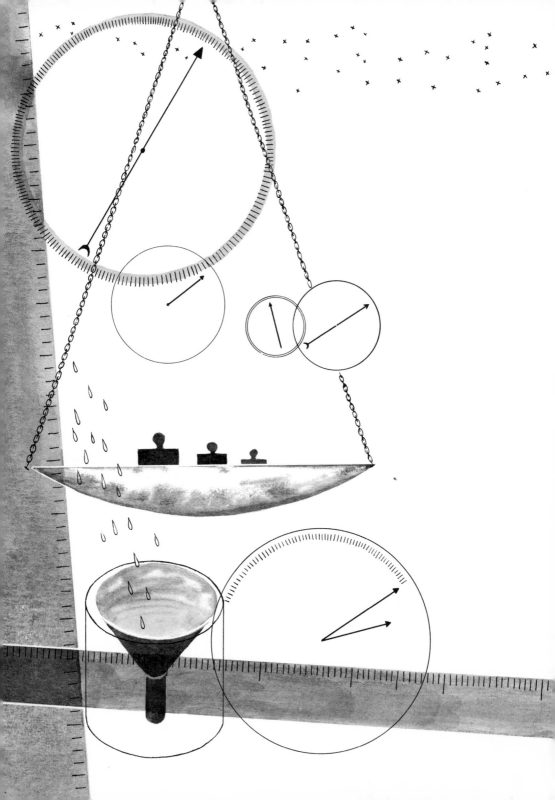

THINGS
THAT
MEASURE

by

PHILIP B. CARONA

illustrated by

JOHN KAUFMANN

PRENTICE-HALL, INC.

ENGLEWOOD CLIFFS, N. J.

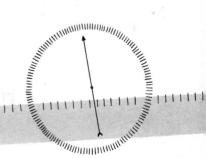

for A. J.

20 19 18 17 16 15 14 13 12 11 10

Things That Measure, by Philip Carona

Library of Congress Catalog Card Number: 62-14742
Printed in the United States of America

91718-T

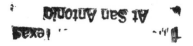

CONTENTS

THINGS

THAT

MEASURE

-1-
SPACE-AGE MEASUREMENT

Within fifty years the world has seen the invention of the airplane and the first manned flight into space!

Things that measure have helped to make the wonders of this space age possible.

Things that measure?

Are you wondering how things that measure helped make a successful journey into space?

Perhaps you have heard stories of large meteorites falling from the sky, but not striking the earth. As they fall, the meteorites are heated white hot by the friction of the air. This usually causes the meteorites to burn and fall apart before reaching the earth.

Heat is a real problem in space travel. Rockets become very hot when moving at great speeds. The heat from the sun also becomes greater as the rockets move farther out into space. To offset this, scientists have developed materials to make rocket "skins" that can withstand the heat caused by the friction of the air. Think what would happen to the nose-cone of a rocket and its pilot, going

9

at the speed of a meteorite if the nose cone could not resist heat. Scientists had to make many measurements of friction, and of the heat caused by friction, before heat-resistant "skins" were made for rockets.

Gravity presents another problem in space travel. When we throw a ball it will always fall to earth. This is so because of the force called gravity. Everything on earth is "pulled" by gravity. Only by getting far enough away from the earth can anything escape this pull.

Have you ever held a needle near a magnet? If you have, you probably remember that the magnet pulled the needle to it. The earth's gravity is like a magnet. The magnet will not draw the needle if the needle is far enough away from the magnet. A rocket zooming toward outer space is very much like the needle. The rocket must "escape" from the earth's gravity in order to reach outer space. Such a rocket must have fuel that can send it beyond the pull of gravity. Through careful measurement and endless experiments we are developing such fuels.

After a very short time in outer space an astronaut finds himself in need of oxygen. Enough oxygen for the astronaut must be stored in the rocket. How much is **enough** oxygen? How can the pilot tell how much oxygen has been used and how much is left? *Gauges*

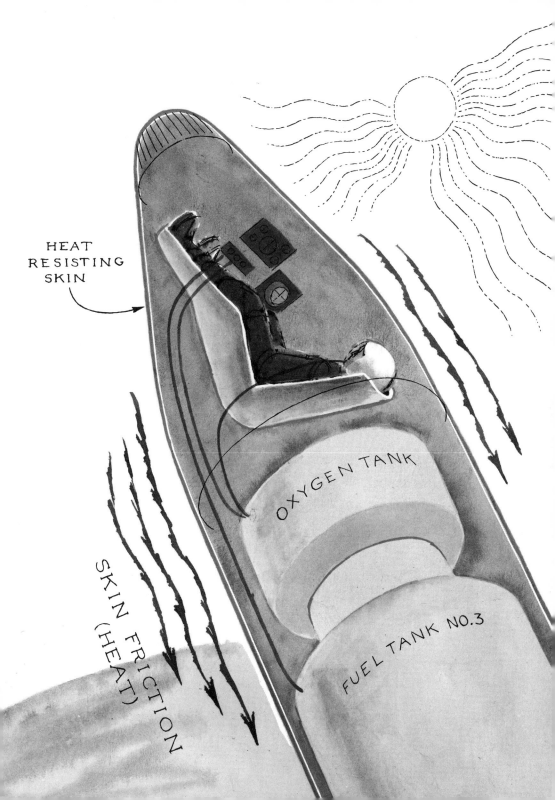

HEAT
RESISTING
SKIN

SKIN FRICTION
(HEAT)

OXYGEN TANK

FUEL TANK NO.3

(*say: GAY-juhs*) and dials tell him. His life depends on these instruments of measure. They must be exact!

During space flight the pilot must wear a pressure suit. The pressure inside the body of the pilot must not be greater than the pressure of the air around him. If it were, the pilot would burst! This is not a happy thought, but it shows the need for wearing a pressure suit. Before a safe pressure suit could be made, there had to be a means of measuring pressure.

Much measuring takes place to help the pilot land the nose cone of a rocket in a small, selected landing area. Radar and other electronic devices have been constructed that make this type of measurement very exact.

Will a trip to the moon be next? Will our pilots journey to the far-away planets of Mars and Venus?

We do not know. But this we can say—the unexplored bodies in space will become easier to reach as we develop more perfect instruments of measure.

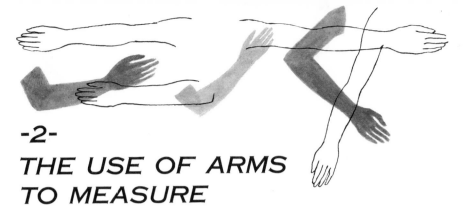

-2-
THE USE OF ARMS TO MEASURE

Today we have scales that can weigh a speck of dust and instruments that can measure the width of a single hair on your head. But when man started measuring things, his methods were very crude.

Do you remember hearing about Noah's Ark? Noah's Ark was said to be three hundred cubits long, fifty cubits wide, and thirty cubits high. But what is a *cubit* (*say: CUE-bit*)?

The cubit is our first known measurement. It is a measurement of length, and represents from seventeen inches to twenty-five inches. The cubit was the measurement of the length of the forearm from the elbow to the tip of the middle finger. This was not an exact measure. Noah's Ark might have been anywhere from one and one-half blocks long to two and one-half blocks long, depending on whose forearm was used as a cubit measure.

Next time you look at a picture of the pyramids of Egypt, it might be well to remember the cubit. The cubit

13

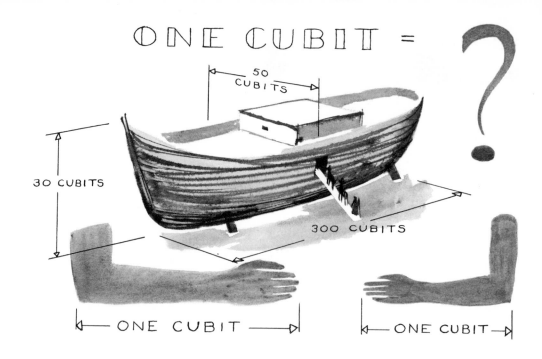

ONE CUBIT = ?

50 CUBITS

30 CUBITS

300 CUBITS

ONE CUBIT

ONE CUBIT

was the basic unit of measurement used in the building of the pyramids.

When we count money, we are measuring. It is simple to measure or count money today (if you have any) because our coins and bills are easy to handle. But early money was often very bulky.

A strange type of money was used long ago by some of the natives of the South Sea Islands. Their money was made from a stone with a hole in the middle. The stones ranged in size from doughnuts to wagon wheels. Can you imagine what would happen today if you and your friends were to enter a supermarket pushing huge stone wheels?

14

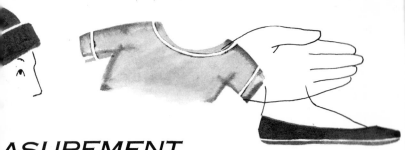

ASUREMENT
OM HEAD TO FOOT

ould probably be very surprised if you knew how
times a day you measured things. There are many
rements we make that we may not consider as
rements.

's take a look into the home. We might start by
g into the cookie jar. That could be one of your
te places. The delicious contents of the cookie
uld not be there without the help of measurement.
g the exact amounts of ingredients is certainly im-
nt in making good cookies. Your mother probably
me measuring cups and spoons to handle this job.
uring cups are divided into ounces. If your mother
eight ounces of milk, she pours until the level in
up reaches the eight-ounce mark. Measuring cups
in different sizes.

ere are different sizes of *measuring* spoons. Some
one half teaspoonful. Some hold one quarter tea-
ful. See how handy this can be when a recipe
for one quarter teaspoonful of salt?

18

Perhaps you would rather "grow" money. Ridiculous?
Well, it is today. But it wasn't in the days when the
state of Virginia was still a colony. There was a time
when Virginia sold so much tobacco to other countries
that tobacco was made legal currency by action of the
Virginian Government. Our coins and bills are certainly
easier to carry than an armful of huge tobacco leaves.

How would you like to go to school each day with a
pocketful of grains, barley or barley corns, as they used
to be called? It might not be much fun, especially if the
barley corns were to be used for measuring. It is much
simpler to rely on a ruler. This leaves your pockets free
for pieces of string, a yo-yo, marbles, a top, or anything
else you might like to put in them. However, many centuries ago, barley corns played an important role in
measurement. It was in 1324, when King Edward II
of England decreed that an inch was the length of
three barley corns taken from the center of an ear of
barley and placed end to end.

STONE MONEY

VIRGINIA
TOBACCO
MONEY

KING HENRY I

KING EDWARD II

King Henry I of England had different ideas about measuring length. He decreed a longer unit of measurement called a *yard*. How was it determined? Well, King Henry said that the distance from the point of his nose to the end of his thumb was the lawful yard. Isn't it much simpler to use a yardstick? Just imagine what it would look like to see a group of boys and girls measuring crepe paper for a school play by holding it up to their noses and extending their arms.

Suppose your mother asked you to light the clock. That's correct—*light the clock!* You might think that your mother wasn't feeling well. Had you been a child living in the ninth century, *lighting* the clock is exactly

16

what you might have done. T
of time made use of a candl
a shadow. The time was kno
shadow.

The old measures discussed
exact. The need for measure
same, or *standardized,* was g

A long time ago, the Rom
of standard weights and meas
when the Roman Empire fell.

Today, we have very accura
measures. In the United State
fixes the standards of weights a
of Standards, in Washington,
units of measure. The standa
is a platinum bar kept by the
check how correct all measuring
paring them with the standard
urements used by people of lon
today's exact measures.

ONE FOOT
STANDARD MEASURE

-3

ME
FR

You
man
mea
mea

L
look
favo
jar
Mix
port
has
Me
need
the
com

T
hold
spo
call

Perhaps you would rather "grow" money. Ridiculous? Well, it is today. But it wasn't in the days when the state of Virginia was still a colony. There was a time when Virginia sold so much tobacco to other countries that tobacco was made legal currency by action of the Virginian Government. Our coins and bills are certainly easier to carry than an armful of huge tobacco leaves.

How would you like to go to school each day with a pocketful of grains, barley or barley corns, as they used to be called? It might not be much fun, especially if the barley corns were to be used for measuring. It is much simpler to rely on a ruler. This leaves your pockets free for pieces of string, a yo-yo, marbles, a top, or anything else you might like to put in them. However, many centuries ago, barley corns played an important role in measurement. It was in 1324, when King Edward II of England decreed that an inch was the length of three barley corns taken from the center of an ear of barley and placed end to end.

STONE MONEY

VIRGINIA
TOBACCO
MONEY

KING HENRY I

KING EDWARD II

King Henry I of England had different ideas about measuring length. He decreed a longer unit of measurement called a *yard*. How was it determined? Well, King Henry said that the distance from the point of his nose to the end of his thumb was the lawful yard. Isn't it much simpler to use a yardstick? Just imagine what it would look like to see a group of boys and girls measuring crepe paper for a school play by holding it up to their noses and extending their arms.

Suppose your mother asked you to light the clock. That's correct—*light the clock!* You might think that your mother wasn't feeling well. Had you been a child living in the ninth century, *lighting* the clock is exactly what you might have done. This measuring instrument of time made use of a candle flame that helped make a shadow. The time was known by the length of the shadow.

The old measures discussed in this chapter were not exact. The need for measurements to be always the same, or *standardized,* was great.

A long time ago, the Romans developed a system of standard weights and measures, but they were lost when the Roman Empire fell.

Today, we have very accurate standard weights and measures. In the United States, for example, Congress fixes the standards of weights and measures. The Bureau of Standards, in Washington, D.C., keeps the standard units of measure. The standard for measuring length is a platinum bar kept by the Bureau. The Bureau can check how correct all measuring instruments are by comparing them with the standard units. The crude measurements used by people of long ago helped us develop today's exact measures.

ONE FOOT
STANDARD MEASURE

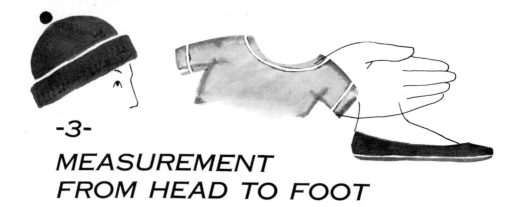

-3-

MEASUREMENT FROM HEAD TO FOOT

You would probably be very surprised if you knew how many times a day you measured things. There are many measurements we make that we may not consider as measurements.

Let's take a look into the home. We might start by looking into the cookie jar. That could be one of your favorite places. The delicious contents of the cookie jar would not be there without the help of measurement. Mixing the exact amounts of ingredients is certainly important in making good cookies. Your mother probably has some measuring cups and spoons to handle this job. *Measuring cups* are divided into ounces. If your mother needs eight ounces of milk, she pours until the level in the cup reaches the eight-ounce mark. Measuring cups come in different sizes.

There are different sizes of *measuring* spoons. Some hold one half teaspoonful. Some hold one quarter teaspoonful. See how handy this can be when a recipe calls for one quarter teaspoonful of salt?

When your mother gets ready to bake the cookies, she must know how long they are to cook. She must also know the amount of heat they should receive. A dial on her range is used to measure the amount of heat the oven will reach. If she didn't have this means of measure, you might have cinders instead of cookies.

The toaster has a heat measuring instrument. Do you like your toast light, medium, or dark? Measuring the amount of heat with a simple dial on the toaster can give you your choice. It's as simple as that.

Much electricity, gas, and water are used in our homes. But yet we know that not all homes use the same amounts. It would not be fair if one family paid as much for their electricity as a family who uses much more. There has to be a method of measuring the amounts

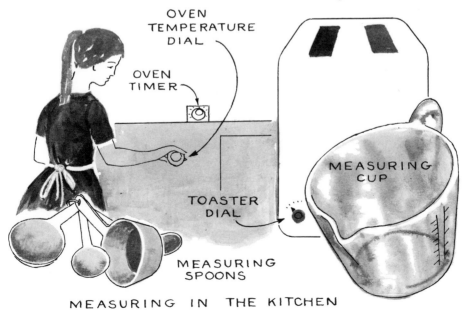

OVEN TEMPERATURE DIAL

OVEN TIMER

TOASTER DIAL

MEASURING CUP

MEASURING SPOONS

MEASURING IN THE KITCHEN

ELECTRIC METER

WATER METER

GAS METER DIALS

of electricity, gas, and water used in each home. The method used is that of *meters*. Meter comes from a Greek word which means measure. A separate meter measures the electricity used in a given period of time. Another meter measures the gas used. Still another meter measures the water that has been used. Each month men from the different utility companies come to your home. They read the meters to see how much electricity, gas, and water have been used. By making these measurements, the companies figure how much money your parents owe them. A bill soon follows the measurements.

When we turn the channel dial on a TV set, we have made a measurement.

When we turn our radio dial to a certain number, we have made a measurement.

When we turn our speed dial on our record player to a certain number, we have made a measurement.

Have you ever worn a pair of shoes that might have been just a little too tight? If so, you probably became the owner of a painful, red blister! How nice, and comfortable, it is to have shoes that have been picked for size after our feet have been properly measured!

The sizes of shirts, pants, dresses, blouses, skirts, and **ALL** clothing are determined by measurement. With regard to clothing, we might say that we use measurements from head to foot! This is a type of measurement that affects our comfort and our health.

There are many instruments of measurement in our automobile. Let's look at a few of them. The *speedometer* (*say: spee-DAHM-uht-r*) measures how fast we are moving. The *odometer* (*say: oh-DAHM-uht-r*) tells us how many miles we have traveled. The *temperature gauge* tells us if our cooling system is working at the temperature it should be. Our *oil gauge* tells us if our oil supply is too low. Another gauge alerts us when our battery is not working properly. Take a close look at an automobile. See how many other things you can find that measure something.

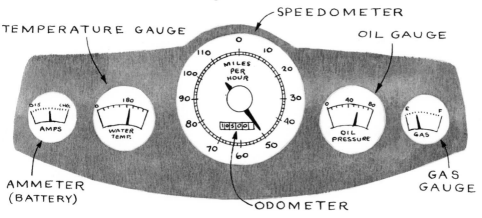

Many of our favorite hobbies involve measurement. If you use a camera, you might use a *light meter* to measure the exact amount of light needed for perfect pictures.

Music involves measurement. In fact, a bar of music is called a *measure*. This is because the number of beats to be played is carefully measured.

An instrument of measure that many musicians use when they practice measures the number of beats in a given period of time. It makes a clicking sound. It is called a *metronome* (*say: MEH-troh-nome*).

Let us make a simple musical instrument that can show us something about measurement. It deals with the measurement of the highness or lowness of a tone, or *pitch*.

Place ten test tubes in line in a test tube rack. Put a small amount of water in the first one. Put a little more water in the second one. Increase the amount of water slightly in each succeeding test tube. With a glass rod lightly tap the first test tube. Listen to the sound. Tap each of the test tubes and listen. Try playing a tune with your musical instrument. Notice that the tubes with shorter air columns give a higher tone. Would this be helpful in measuring how solid or hollow some objects might be?

MEASURE | MEASURE | MEASURE

3 BEATS   3 BEATS   3 BEATS

METRONOME

PITCH
EXPERIMENT

LOW   HIGH

MEASUREMENT IN MUSIC

-4-
THE RULER IS THE RULER

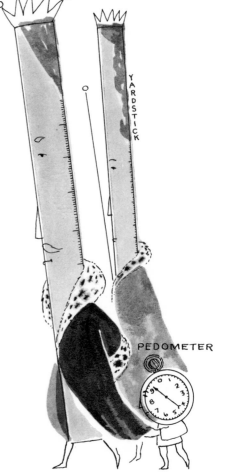

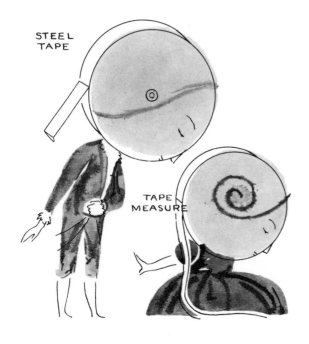

STEEL TAPE

TAPE MEASURE

YARDSTICK

PEDOMETER

You may want to know the length of a piece of wire or a piece of jump rope.

A ruler will help you find out such things. Measuring length is something most of us need to do very often. The most common instrument we use for measuring length is the ruler. The ruler is such a common instrument for measuring length that we might call it the ruler in the kingdom of length measuring instruments.

Most rulers are one foot long. The most common type of ruler is divided into twelve inches. The divisions are shown by marks and numbers. There are usually markings between each inch, dividing each inch into several equal parts. Sometimes the inches are divided into four, eight, or sixteen equal parts. This helps us to be more exact in our measurements.

In measuring lengths longer than one foot, we find it helpful to use a longer ruler. This ruler is three feet long instead of one foot long. Since there are three feet in one yard, we call this long ruler a *yardstick*. Have you ever tried measuring the distance all the way round your classroom? A yardstick would be a good instrument to use for this job.

Next time your mother is sewing, you might see her measure length with a ruler made of cloth. Its rulings are marked on cloth that looks like tape. This kind of ruler is called a *tape measure*. It is easy to handle and can be rolled up and placed in a very small space when it isn't being used.

Measuring land would be a very slow job if small rulers were used. The men who measure land use a type of ruler that winds into a case. The case can be held with one hand. The ruler is made of thin steel, and we usually call it a *steel tape*. Steel tapes come in different lengths. Some are fifty feet long. Some are one hundred feet long. The tape can be pulled by one person while another person holds the case. A steel tape would be a good instrument to use to measure the length of your home.

Have you ever been on a hike? If so, you might have walked a long distance. Maybe you were interested in knowing just how far you really did walk! There is a simple way of measuring how far you walk. A measuring instrument called a *pedometer* (*say: pih-DAHM-uht-r*) can measure the distance. A pedometer looks like a small clock. You can place it on your belt. As you walk, the pedometer clicks and keeps the record of the distance you are hiking.

Wearing a ring that doesn't fit can be most uncomfortable. If it is too tight, it will hurt. If it is too loose, you might lose it. The right size ring for you is easy to find if an exact measurement is made. Suppose you want a new ring, and you want it to be made exactly the same size as your old ring. The jeweler can place your old ring on a *jeweler's stick*. This stick is tapered so that the old ring can be placed at the point where an exact measurement can be made. He reads the measurement and

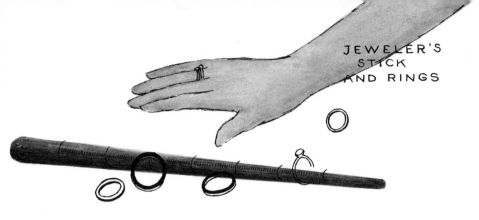

makes your ring exactly the same size as your old ring. If you do not have an old ring, he can measure your size by letting you put your ring finger in several rings that have already been measured. They are marked with numbers. When you find the proper size, he will read the measurement of that ring.

Measurement also plays an important role in athletics. A football play can be so exciting, especially when it's fourth down and only inches away from a first down! Think of the hush in the stands when the linesmen are making this important measurement! If the team can carry the ball ten yards in four plays, they get another first down! This makes it necessary to have a measuring device that is ten yards long. The linesmen use a ten-yard long piece of chain to make the measurements. The linesmen must be very careful because a mistake in measurement could cost a team a game victory.

Next time you look at a volleyball, basketball, or tennis court, notice the markings on the court. The markings

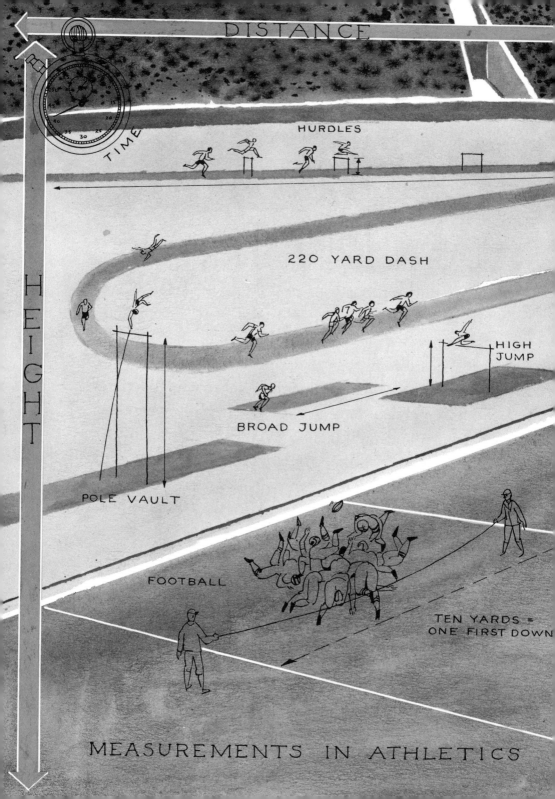

DISTANCE

TIME

HURDLES

220 YARD DASH

HIGH JUMP

BROAD JUMP

POLE VAULT

HEIGHT

FOOTBALL

TEN YARDS = ONE FIRST DOWN

MEASUREMENTS IN ATHLETICS

are very important to the rules of the games. The markings show measurements of length from many parts of the court. It would be impossible to play the game by the rules if the courts were not properly measured and marked.

"On your mark—get set—GO!" Those are inviting words if you like to race. Before you can have a race, though, you must have a *distance* to race. You might run from one tree to another tree in your yard at home. You might run from one bush to another bush in your friend's yard. If you were being timed to see how fast you could run, you would have to know the exact distance to compare your timings. A steel tape can truly be a friend in need in solving this problem. Before you can know exactly how fast you can run, you must have accurate measuring instruments: one to measure *time*, another to measure *distance*. An accurate watch will measure the time. An accurate steel tape will measure the distance.

You might also use the steel tape in measuring how far you can jump.

You will find that you use ways of measuring length very often.

-5-

HALF FULL
OR HALF EMPTY?

Suppose you are doing a science experiment, and you want to use a very small amount of liquid. You want to use much less than a teaspoonful. How are you going to measure it? An instrument that might be just what you need is the *eyedropper*. By filling the eyedropper, and squeezing the bulb, you can measure your liquid in drops. That is certainly getting to measuring small amounts! Many times medicine is given in terms of drops.

If you want to measure a larger amount of liquid, you might use a flask or a beaker. A *flask* is a type of bottle designed to hold liquids. A *beaker* is a type of glass. It looks much like a drinking glass except that it may have a pouring lip. Beakers and flasks come in many different sizes. Each size is designed to hold a certain amount of liquid.

After pouring some maple-flavored syrup on your waffles, you might decide that the bottle of syrup is half full. Yet, you might realize that the bottle is also half empty. Whether you decide to say the bottle is half full or half empty, you really mean the same thing. But you aren't really telling just how much syrup is left! The bottle may be a small bottle or it may be a large bottle. The bottle is not a standard measurement. There are many sizes and shapes of bottles having different capacities. *Capacity* (*say: kuh-PASS-uh-tee*) tells us how much something will hold. A common type of bottle is the one used to hold one *quart* of milk. A milk bottle half that size is called a *pint*. So there are two pints in one quart. A giant-size bottle that will hold four quarts is a *gallon*. How many days would it take you to drink a gallon of milk?

On a cold winter day perhaps you enjoy a cup of hot chocolate topped with whipped cream. You might even like a giant-sized cup. While there are different sizes of cups, the most popular size of cup is one that will hold one-half pint. Since there are sixteen ounces in a pint, the cup holds eight ounces of liquid.

EYEDROPPER

FLASK

BEAKER

D R Y

 BUSHEL = **4**  PECKS

 PECK = **8** QUARTS

L I Q U I D

 CUP = = 8 OUNCES

½ PINT

 PINT = **2**  CUPS = 16 OUNCES

QUART = **2** PINTS = 32 OUNCES

 GALLON = **4** QUARTS = 128 OUNCES

DRY AND LIQUID MEASURE

To see many liquid measurements made, all you would have to do is spend about an hour at a busy filling station. A statement heard very often around a filling station is, "Ten gallons of gas, please." Perhaps your father has said that many times. The man at the filling station does not need a gallon container to measure the gasoline going into your family car. He has a *meter gasoline tank.* As the gasoline leaves the storage tank and enters the tank of the car, a meter shows how many gallons of gasoline are being poured. The meter also shows how much the gasoline costs. Just think about that! A meter that tells not only the number of gallons, but also the cost. That meter is certainly a worker in arithmetic!

While we have discussed some of the objects to measure amounts of liquids, we should also think about the instruments that measure solids. When we measure a solid, we are making a *dry measurement.* A quart of ice cream is a dry measurement. In some places, people may buy fruit or vegetables by the *peck.* A peck is much larger than a quart. In fact, it is eight times as much! Perhaps your mother likes to make peach preserves. If so, she probably preserves a large number of peaches at one time. She might buy a bushel at a time. A bushel of peaches will hold as many peaches as four pecks will. That's a lot of peaches!

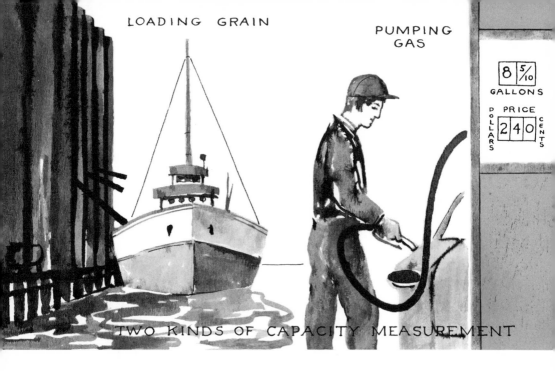

LOADING GRAIN

PUMPING GAS

8 5/10 GALLONS

DOLLARS PRICE CENTS
2 4 0

TWO KINDS OF CAPACITY MEASUREMENT

Have you ever heard about ships being loaded with thousands of bushels of certain products? If so, you more than likely wondered how the ships were loaded. Perhaps the job of loading is sometimes faster than you realize. Since the United States ships a great amount of grain to foreign countries, let us imagine a huge ship being loaded with grain. Think of the ship being docked near a large grain storehouse, or grain elevator. A large vacant area of the ship is to be filled with grain. Giant spouts that look like cannon extend from the grain elevator. They are pointed toward the storage hold of the ship. The grain comes rushing through the spouts!

The grain comes through the spouts so fast that a light dust spreads through the loading area. What was an empty space in the ship is shortly filled with grain. In just a few hours the section of the ship to be loaded is practically full. The roaring of the cannons, or spouts, stops when the proper capacity has been reached. In nearly a few hours, it is possible to deliver thousands and thousands of bushels of grain to the ship.

You need only visit several types of stores in your neighborhood to see many instruments used to hold and measure dry and liquid materials. You might try visiting the supermarket, the paint store, the filling station, and the pharmacy. A pleasant way to end your visit might be to have a cold, frosted, eight-ounce bottle of your favorite soda water. Eight ounces—one half pint—one cup, remember? Oh, well, they're the same amounts anyway.

-6-

HOW MUCH WOULD YOU WEIGH ON THE MOON?

Suppose you weigh sixty pounds. If you could take a trip to the moon, you would discover that you weighed less on the moon. You would weigh only about ten pounds on the moon. On the planet Mars you would weigh about twenty-two pounds. On the planet Saturn you would weigh about seventy pounds. How can this be?

Earlier we talked about the strong force of *gravity*. Gravity is always pulling on everything. It is gravity that makes the weighing of things possible. All heavenly bodies pull objects towards them. In fact, every object pulls on all other objects. But the force of gravity on earth is stronger than the gravity of some of the other heavenly bodies. Some planets have gravity that is stronger than earth's gravity. Some planets have gravity that is weaker than earth's gravity. You would not weigh the same amount on another planet as you weigh on earth.

Perhaps you have weighed yourself many times. May-

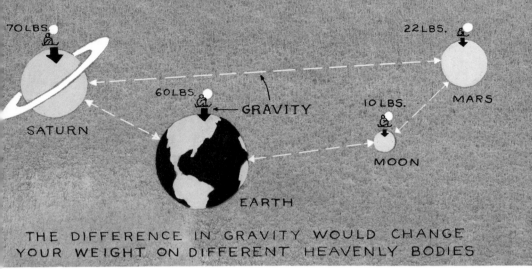

70 LBS.

22 LBS.

60 LBS.
GRAVITY

10 LBS.
MARS

SATURN

MOON

EARTH

THE DIFFERENCE IN GRAVITY WOULD CHANGE
YOUR WEIGHT ON DIFFERENT HEAVENLY BODIES

be you have weighed other objects, such as a piece of
metal, or a fish that you caught. Let us do an experiment
in weighing something *invisible*. We will weigh some
air!

All we need is a simple spring scale, a football, and
an air pump.

Release the air from the football and attach it to the
spring scale. Read how much the football weighs, and
record the weight.

Remove the football and fill it with air by using the
hand-type air pump. Attach the football to the scale and
take a reading. Record the weight. Notice that this reading is greater than the first reading. What caused this
reading to be greater? The weight of the football did
not change. The added weight is the weight of the air
you put into the football. Subtract the first reading from

1. WEIGH EMPTY FOOTBALL

2. PUMP UP BALL

3. WEIGH BALL AGAIN

4. SUBTRACT FIRST WEIGH FROM SECOND. THIS DIFFERENCE GIVES THE WEIGHT OF THE AIR IN THE BALL.

AN EXPERIMENT IN WEIGHING AIR

the second reading and you have the weight of the air you put into the football.

With today's modern instruments of measuring weight, we are able to measure the exact weight of the largest elephant alive! We can also measure the weight of the smallest ant you have ever seen! Of course, you may never need or even want to measure either an elephant or an ant, but you may want to weigh yourself.

Suppose you weighed sixty pounds on one scale, fifty pounds on another scale, and forty pounds on still another scale. You would be quite puzzled as to your exact weight. It is important that we observe our weight from time to time because proper weight is essential to good health.

Proper weight is easily determined because our scales of today are very exact. Have you ever been weighed on the scale in your family doctor's office? He probably has a scale that will measure your weight to the nearest half-pound. His scale might even divide a pound into four or more equal parts. It is inspected often to make sure that it is giving exact weights.

A scale that can weigh an object much heavier than any man is a *platform* scale. A platform scale can weigh an automobile, a carload of coal, or an airplane.

The chemist and the pharmacist have to make many weight measurements of small amounts. Many chemicals and drugs weigh only a matter of grains. How heavy is a *grain*? Perhaps this will give you some idea. There are 437½ grains in one ounce. Most candy bars weigh between one and two ounces. That makes a grain a very small amount of weight, doesn't it? Yet, there are many medicines that call for only a few grains of certain substances. If the substances were not measured to the exact amounts, the medicine could be a killer! So you see, exact measuring in the making of medicine can be a matter of life and death!

Getting proper amounts and kinds of food is also a matter of life and death. Today's modern supermarkets have quite a variety of wonderful, delicious foods. Many of today's supermarkets have fruits, vegetables, and meats packaged and displayed. They are ready for the customer to purchase. This saves the customer much

ANCIENT EGYPT

time. It also helps the grocer manage his time more wisely. But how does the customer know she is getting sixteen ounces (one full pound) of ground meat instead of fourteen ounces? This is a very simple thing with the aid of today's weight-measuring instruments. The modern supermarket scale weighed the object at the time of packing. A printing device in the scale recorded the weight on a strip of paper. The printing showed the weight of the object, and also the cost for that particular amount of the object. This small strip of paper has a light glue on one side so that it is easily attached to the package holding the product. There are laws that require the stores to have their scales checked often enough to make sure that they are working properly.

Weighing the largest, the smallest, the visible, and the invisible are all things that can be done with the weight-measuring instruments of today.

ANCIENT SYRIAN BALANCE

PLATFORM SCALES

MARKET PRINTER SCALE

INDIAN BALANCE SCALE

SCIENCE

MEDICINE

DOCTOR'S
SCALE

PRECISION BEAM BALANCE

THINGS THAT MEASURE WEIGHT

-7-
ONLY
SECONDS AWAY

What time does school start? When is your birthday? How much longer before vacation time? Question after question can be asked about time. Can you imagine what would happen if our time-measuring instruments were not exact?

Many centuries ago, the Hindus had the sad experience of dividing the year by guesswork. The priests chose the number of days there were to be in each year. Sometimes they set the number of days at 324. But they were just as likely to decide that a year would have 378 days.

If we were to use this ancient Hindu method of setting the days of the year, we might very well have Christmas day during the peak of the summer and celebrate the Fourth of July during the cold winter!

The ancient Egyptians were more exact than the Hindus. More than three thousand years ago they noticed that a certain star would return to the same position in the sky after a period of time had passed.

They counted the days from the time the star was in one position until it was in the same position again. They found that this took 365 days.

This knowledge led to the invention of a *calendar* (this word comes from a Latin word meaning "account book"). The Egyptian year had 365 days. They divided their year into twelve months, with thirty days in each month. The left-over days were placed at the end of the year as "feast days."

Our calendar is based on our observations of the earth and its relation to the sun. Our earth is constantly spinning like a top, or *rotating* (*say: ROE-tayt-ing*).

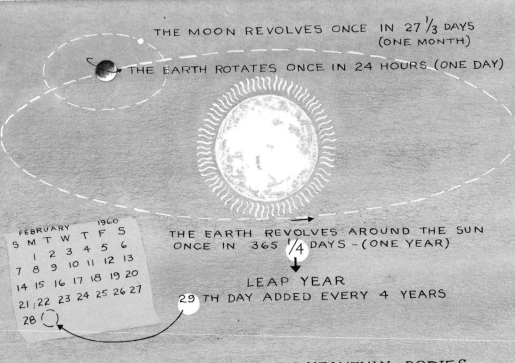

THE MOON REVOLVES ONCE IN 27 1/3 DAYS (ONE MONTH)

THE EARTH ROTATES ONCE IN 24 HOURS (ONE DAY)

FEBRUARY 1960
S M T W T F S
1 2 3 4 5 6
7 8 9 10 11 12 13
14 15 16 17 18 19 20
21 22 23 24 25 26 27
28

THE EARTH REVOLVES AROUND THE SUN ONCE IN 365 1/4 DAYS – (ONE YEAR)

LEAP YEAR
29 TH DAY ADDED EVERY 4 YEARS

HOW TIME IS MEASURED BY HEAVENLY BODIES

The earth rotates once every twenty-four hours. While our half of the earth is facing the sun it is daylight for us, but it is night time for the other half of the earth which is facing away from the sun in darkness. Besides rotating, our earth is turning around the sun, or *revolving* (*say: re-VAULV-ing*). It goes completely around the sun every 365¼ days. This is a period of one year.

Because a full year does not have a number of days ending in a whole number, the designer of our calendar had to find a way to handle the ¼ day which was left over each year.

The problem was solved in this manner: The calendar allows 30 days each for the months of September, April, June, and November. It allows 31 days for the remaining months, except February. The month of February has 28 days. Adding the days in each month throughout the year, you will get a total of 365 days. Now, for the problem of the ¼ day left over each year! By adding one full day to the month of February each fourth year, we actually add ¼ day to each year. There is our solution! We call the year in which February has 29 days, *leap year*. A year is a leap year if its number can be divided exactly by 4. The year 1964 and 2000 are leap years; 1963 is not.

Long before man invented the calendar he learned

to tell the time of day by the sun and the shadows it casts. Look at the shadow cast by the flag pole at your school on a sunny morning. Then look at the shadow it casts later in the day and you will see that the shadow is in a different position than it was in the morning.

Positions of shadows at different times of the day helped man to use the sun as a kind of clock. From his observations of shadows cast by the sun man developed a kind of clock called a sun dial.

Let us travel back into time and examine a sundial. We will examine it by making one!

To make a sun dial, place a large sheet of tag board or light-colored cardboard in a place that is sunny all day. Construct a large circle on the tag board. Drive a thin pole into the ground, first passing through the

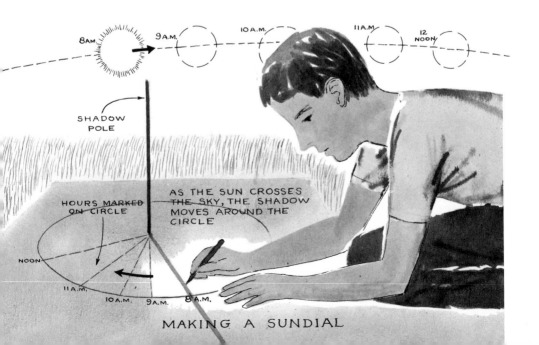

MAKING A SUNDIAL

tag board, at the center of the large circle you constructed.

Notice the shadow of the pole.

Each hour, go to your sun dial and mark the correct time on the circle where the shadow strikes.

You will be able to use this sun dial to tell time for several days. The position of the sun with relation to the earth is not exactly the same at a given hour each day. If it were, we would not have seasons of the year. For that reason, you cannot use the sundial in the same position all year round. To use it for longer periods of time, you might make new numbers on your dial about every ten days. In other words, you will have to reset your clock.

The invention of the mechanical clock was one of the greatest advances in the history of time-measuring instruments. Many people feel that a French monk named *Gerbert* (*say: zhair-BARE*), invented the first mechanical clock.

Today, we have clocks that are made in many shapes and sizes. They can be operated mechanically or electrically. Some are highly decorated while others are very simple.

A watch is a very small clock. Peter *Henlein* (*say: HEN-line*), a German clock maker, receives credit for making the first watches. He invented the mainspring. The *mainspring* in a watch is actually the source of energy. It is a small, metal, coiled spring. The energy of the spring is released in small amounts at exact intervals. The time is measured by counting the intervals and registering the total on a watch dial.

Stop-watches and *timers* are types of watches used to measure small periods of time.

Today, one can find a watch or a clock to handle many time-measuring jobs.

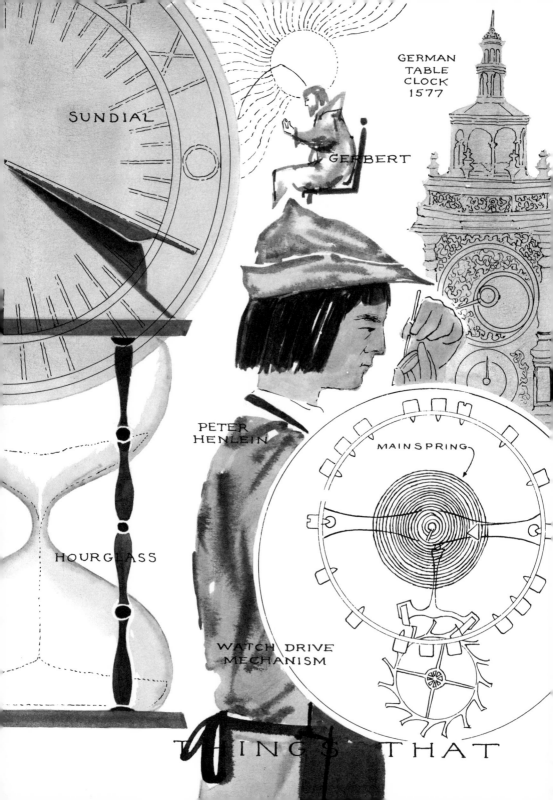

SUNDIAL

GERMAN
TABLE
CLOCK
1577

GERBERT

PETER
HENLEIN

MAINSPRING

HOURGLASS

WATCH DRIVE
MECHANISM

THINGS THAT

AMERICAN LONGCASE CLOCK
1790

PHOTOGRAPHIC
DARKROOM
TIMER

STOPWATCH

EGG
TIMER

WRISTWATCH

MEASURE TIME

-8-

A REPORT ON TOMORROW'S WEATHER TODAY

In September, 1961, a terrible hurricane lashed part of the Gulf Coast of Texas. *Hurricane Carla's* destructive wind reached a speed of 125 miles per hour! Had it not been for excellent weather forecasting and reporting, thousands of lives might have been lost. As it was, there were very few deaths and injuries.

So you see, the main value of excellent weather predicting and reporting is protecting the lives of people.

Weather forecasting also protects much property. We would lose many of our orange and grapefruit crops in Texas, California, and Florida, if it were not for the services of the United States Weather Bureau. Citrus fruits cannot stand extremely cold weather. The fruit growers know when a hard freeze is coming. They listen carefully to the weather reports. If a hard freeze is on the way, they can burn fuel in huge pots that are located in the orchards. This keeps the temperature in the orchards high enough to save the fruit. Maybe the weather bureau helped save the next orange you eat.

To make sound weather predictions, the weather bureau must make many measurements.

The direction of the wind is important. This measure is made by using a *wind vane.* The wind vane is a large arrow attached to a pole in such a way that the arrow can revolve. The wind moves the arrow so that the point of the arrow will show the direction of the wind.

The speed of the wind is also important. Measurement with an *anemometer* (*say: an-uh-MOM-uh-tuhr*) takes care of this job. A system of cups are attached to a pole so that they can revolve. Each cup is shaped like half of a hollow ball. As the wind strikes the cups, this section of the anemometer revolves. The faster the wind moves, the faster this section revolves. The speed of the wind can be read directly from the gauge.

When we talk about hot weather or cold weather, we are really talking about the temperature of the air. To measure the temperature of the air, we use an instrument called a *thermometer* (*say: thur-MOM-uh-tuhr*). A thermometer is a thin glass tube with some colored alcohol or mercury in it. As the air gets hotter, the liquid in the tube expands and goes higher up the tube. As the air cools, the liquid in the tube drops its level. Numbers on the material holding the tube make it easy for us to read the temperature.

One of the most important measurements in making weather predictions is measuring the pressure of the air. The *barometer* (*say: buh-ROM-uh-tuhr*) measures air pressure. There are different types of barometers. Let us look at one of them. It works because air presses down on a cup of mercury. Mercury is a heavy, silvery, liquid metal. As air presses down on the mercury, some of the mercury rises in the tube. The greater the air pressure, the higher the mercury will rise in the tube. Numbers marked on a frame holding the tube make it easy to read the pressure of the air.

Rainfall is measured with a *rain gauge*. The rain gauge is a tube with inches marked on the outside. The gauge is placed where the rainfall will strike it. Some of the water enters the gauge. When it stops raining, the level of the water in the gauge is measured by reading the figure. Simple, isn't it?

There are many more instruments that help with this big job of weather predicting. They all play a part in helping us learn something about tomorrow's weather today.

By carefully following the instructions below, YOU can make a REAL weather-measuring instrument. It is a type of thermometer.

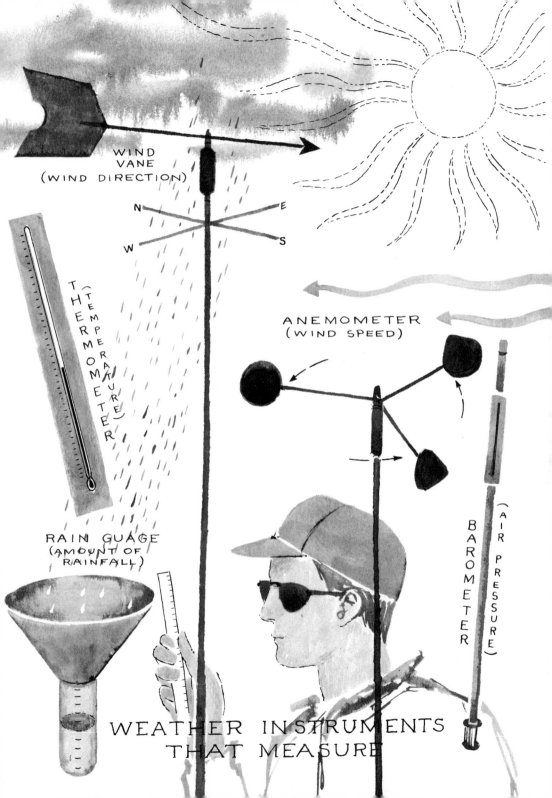

WIND VANE
(WIND DIRECTION)

N   E
W   S

THERMOMETER
(TEMPERATURE)

ANEMOMETER
(WIND SPEED)

RAIN GUAGE
(AMOUNT OF
RAINFALL)

BAROMETER
(AIR PRESSURE)

WEATHER INSTRUMENTS
THAT MEASURE

Get a bottle. It doesn't matter what size you use. A pint milk bottle would be very easy to work with. You will need a one-hole rubber stopper to fit the bottle. You will also need a piece of glass tubing bent as shown in the illustration. Place the glass tubing through the hole in the rubber stopper. Fit the stopper into the bottle. Color some water with ink, and half fill a drinking glass with it.

After your materials have been set up as they are in the illustration, place a hot wet towel around the bottle. You will notice the colored water from the glass will rise in the tube after the hot towel is removed from the bottle. As the temperature increases, the liquid in the

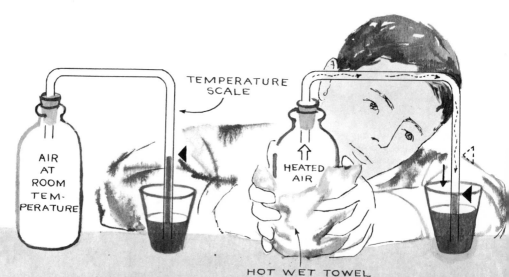

MAKING YOUR OWN THERMOMETER

tube goes down. The heat forces air out of the bottle, and pushes the column of liquid down.

You might print a temperature scale on the glass tube. White or black paint would be good to use. Look at a regular thermometer and use the same numbers on your scale. You will be able to read the temperature each day.

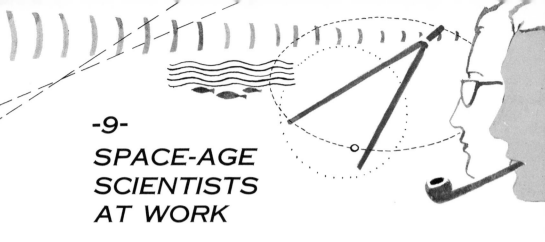

-9-
SPACE-AGE SCIENTISTS AT WORK

There are many kinds of scientists. They work with different materials and equipment—but every one of them measures something, usually many things.

Some scientists work in space laboratories. Among other things, they measure the speed of jet airplanes. They have even measured the speed of sound. Scientists know that at room temperature, sound travels in air at over 1,100 feet in one second! How amazing to realize that we have jet planes that can travel much faster than the speed of sound! When a jet plane is traveling faster than the speed of sound, it can cause a huge wave of sound to strike the earth. It sounds like a giant blast! It is called a sonic boom.

While the speed of sound is very fast, it is a slow traveler compared to light. The speed of light has been measured to be 186,000 MILES per second! Light can travel over seven times the distance around the earth in one second! That makes even modern rockets seem slow-moving!

Some of the stars are billions and billions of miles away. To measure their distance in miles would mean that we would have to use very big numbers. We make this job easier by describing the long distances in terms of light years. A *light year* is the distance that light travels in one year! In number of miles, that would be about 6,000,000,000,000 miles, or 6 trillion miles!

On July 1, 1957, an interesting scientific venture started. Scientists from sixty-seven different countries joined efforts to make many scientific observations and measurements. The period was to end on December 31, 1958. It was called the *International Geophysical Year,* or *I. G. Y.* In our usual measurement of time the International Geophysical Year was actually a year and a half. However, plans were changed to make it last for ten years, or a *decade* (*say: DEK-ade*).

The laboratories of the I. G. Y. scientists were the upper atmosphere, the lower atmosphere and surface, and the inside of the earth.

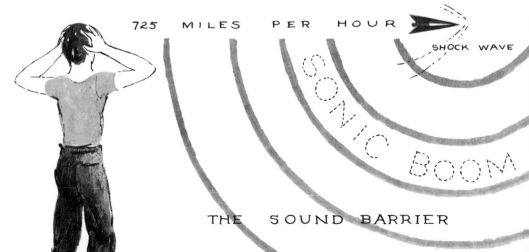

725 MILES PER HOUR

SHOCK WAVE

SONIC BOOM

THE SOUND BARRIER

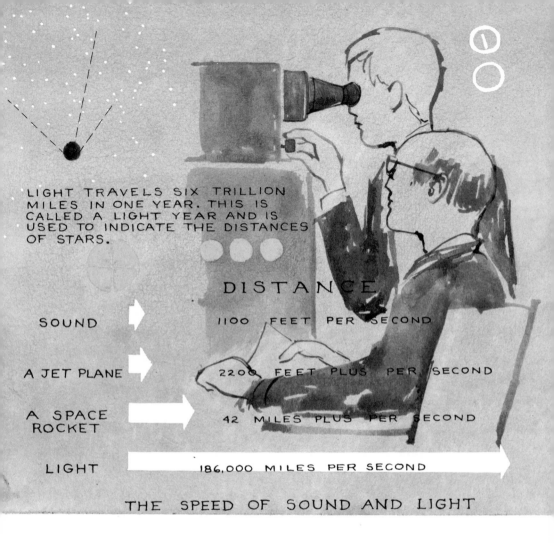

LIGHT TRAVELS SIX TRILLION MILES IN ONE YEAR. THIS IS CALLED A LIGHT YEAR AND IS USED TO INDICATE THE DISTANCES OF STARS.

DISTANCE

SOUND	1100 FEET PER SECOND
A JET PLANE	2200 FEET PLUS PER SECOND
A SPACE ROCKET	42 MILES PLUS PER SECOND
LIGHT	186,000 MILES PER SECOND

THE SPEED OF SOUND AND LIGHT

One interesting achievement since the beginning of I. G. Y. is that artificial earth satellites have been orbited. With them we have been able to make many measurements of temperature at high altitudes. Satellites have also helped measure very small meteorites believed to be debris left over from the formation of our solar system.

Scientists made many measurements in oceans. They were able to recover a small shellfish alive at an ocean depth of about two and a half miles. A worm, a quarter of an inch long, was recovered alive at a depth of about three miles.

Will discoveries of sea animals at great ocean depths lead to a new era in obtaining food from the sea? Perhaps there are delicious seafoods deep in the ocean that we do not know about. They might be there in great abundance.

An underwater mountain range of five thousand feet high was discovered on the floor of the Arctic Ocean. This range is higher than the tallest mountain on land.

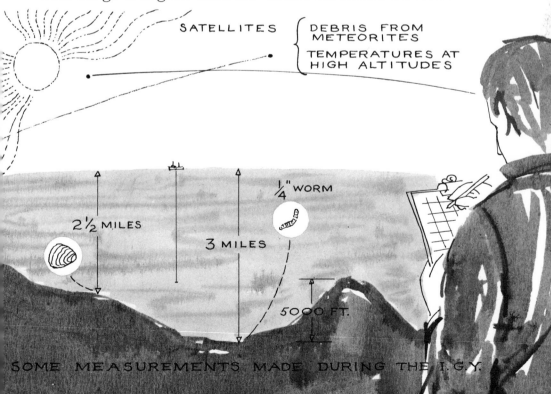

SATELLITES { DEBRIS FROM METEORITES
TEMPERATURES AT HIGH ALTITUDES

2½ MILES

¼" WORM

3 MILES

5000 FT.

SOME MEASUREMENTS MADE DURING THE I. G. Y.

We will certainly learn more about our earth's surface as we learn more about what is under the ocean. It may be that underwater mountain ranges are great storehouses of valuable minerals. If so, our scientists may discover methods of obtaining the minerals that are stored below the water. We already know that the oceans contain many minerals. In fact, some industries are now beginning to recover minerals from large bodies of water. An interesting example of this is the recovery of a light metal called *magnesium* (*say: mag-NEE-shi-um*) from the Gulf of Mexico. This useful metal is now recovered in abundance from the water and is stored in large blocks, called *ingots* (*say: ING-uts*).

Scientists also know that there is much gold in the waters of the oceans. The process for recovering the gold is so expensive that it has not been practical to go after it. Perhaps some day scientists will find a way to recover the gold that will make it worthwhile. This very method might be discovered during the International Geophysical Decade!

As the scientists continue their observations and measurements, perhaps new areas of science will be opened through the results of the International Geophysical Decade.

-10-
LOOKING AHEAD!

Do you think that the time is coming when an elementary school student can take a field trip to Europe in one day? Think of that! You arrive at your school on the East Coast at 8:30 A.M. You make a rocket flight to London, a visit to many of London's interesting sights, and back to your school in time to go home promptly at three. Fantastic? Maybe, and maybe not.

Perhaps when our grandparents were children, they dreamed of artificial earth satellites. Perhaps they thought such objects were fantastic. Today, there are many such satellites.

Perhaps we are not far away from having wrist-band TV sets. A real TV unit shaped like a wrist watch. Incredible? Maybe, and maybe not. From the old, bulky radio sets of many years ago we have made radio units that can fit into a kitchen match box. The making of the tiny transistor has helped bring this about.

SOLAR PUMPING ENGINE

Maybe we will have bicycles that we won't have to pedal. A small unit run by solar energy will make them move. Ridiculous? Maybe, and maybe not. Scientists have already successfully made engines that can be operated by the sun's energy.

One could go on and on thinking about things that might become realities. While no one can foretell the future, using the imagination often makes the most fantastic ideas work.

One of the main things that brings about new inventions and discoveries is the *need* for them. If people have a greater need for something, more scientists work on the problem. They spend more time trying to solve the problem. People contribute more money to solution of the problem. A good example of this can be found in the development of the polio *vaccines* (*say: VAK-seens*). Polio is a disease that once crippled many people. The need for something to fight this disease was very great. Many scientists worked to find a vaccine. Much time was devoted to the problem. Much money was contributed to help find the answer. In time safe, sure vaccines were made.

As time goes on, we will have additional needs. Scientists will work hard to find the solutions to many problems. There is one thing for sure—whatever the problem is, somebody, somewhere, will be using—THINGS THAT MEASURE!

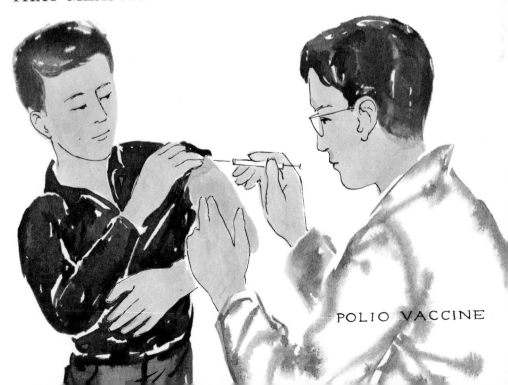

POLIO VACCINE

Glossary

abacus (say: *AB-uh-kus*)   an instrument for working out arithmetical problems, made of beads strung on wires set in a frame.

A. D.   the abbreviation for *Anno Domini,* Latin for: in the Year of Our Lord.

altimeter (say: *al-TIM-uh-tr*)   an instrument for measuring the height at which an airplane is flying.

ammeter (say: *AM-me-tr*)   an instrument for measuring electric current.

ampere (say: *AM-pihr*)   a unit of electric current.

audiometer (say: *ah-dih-AHM-uh-tr*)   an instrument for measuring hearing.

avoirdupois (say: *av-uhr-duh-POYZ*)   a system of weights commonly used in English-speaking countries for weighing everything except precious stones, precious metals, and drugs. In this system there are 16 ounces to the pound.

barograph   a self-recording barometer. This instrument makes a recording on a piece of paper of the atmospheric pressure.

B. C.   abbreviation for *Before Christ.*

calorie   a unit of heat. A calorie is the amount of heat required to raise the temperature of a gram of water one degree centigrade.

carat   a twenty-fourth part. This word is used in stating the fineness of gold. 24 carat gold is pure gold. Fourteen carat gold is 14 parts gold and 10 parts of other metal.

chronometer (say: *kruh-NAHM-uh-tr*)   a special kind of clock used on ships.

circumference   the distance around a circle.

Daylight Saving Time   a system of setting the clocks back for one hour in the summer to provide more hours of daylight while awake. This system is used in many states.

Decimal system of money   our system of money with the unit being the dollar. There are 100 cents in a dollar and 10 dimes in a dollar.

dew point   the temperature at which the water vapor in the air begins to condense.

diameter   the distance through the center of a circle.

druggists' weights   very tiny weights based on the troy ounce. They are used by druggists.

Fahrenheit (say: *FAR-uhn-hite*) **System**   a system of measuring temperature where the freezing point of water is 32 degrees and the boiling point of water is 212 degrees.

fathom   a measure of length containing six feet.

66

fathometer   an instrument used to measure the distance from the surface of a body of water to the bottom.

frequency   the number of times per second that something vibrates.

furlong   a measure of length equaling 220 yards.

grain   in apothecaries' weights, or druggists' weights, the grain is a unit of weight. There are 20 grains in one *scruple.*

gram   the unit of weight in the metric system. All other units of weight in the metric system are made by dividing or multiplying a gram by 10 or any multiple of ten.

Geiger (say: *GUY-gr*) **counter**   an instrument that detects and measures atomic radiation.

Greenwich (say: *GREN-itch*) **Standard Time**   The time kept in the Greenwich, England, Time Zone is the standard time for the whole world. This is the time kept in the zone along the Zero Meridian. All other zones take their time from the time kept in the Greenwich Zone.

horsepower   a unit of work. James Watt found that a strong horse could, by means of a rope and pulley, pull a 150-pound weight out of a coal pit through a distance of 220 feet in one minute. This amount of work is called *one horsepower.*

hour glass   an instrument for measuring time. A quantity of sand runs between two glass bulbs in just one hour.

hygrometer (say: *high-GRAWM-uh-tr*)   an instrument that can measure the relative humidity of the air.

67

International Bureau of Weights and Measures   a Bureau in France that houses the world's official metric standards: a cylinder made of platinum and iridium, weighing exactly one kilogram, and a platinum and iridium bar marked to show exactly the length of one meter.

kilogram (say: *KIL-uh-gram*)   1,000 grams.

kilometer (say: *KIL-uh-me-tr*)   1,000 meters.

kiloton (say: *KIL-uh-ton*)   a unit of blasting power equal to the blasting power of 1,000 tons of TNT.

kindling temperature   the temperature at which a substance will catch on fire.

liter (say: *LEE-tr*)   a metric unit of capacity. In liquid measurement, this unit is slightly more than a quart.

megaton   a thousand kilotons, or the blasting power of a million tons of TNT.

meter   a unit of length in the metric system. This length is a little more than 39⅓ inches.

metric system   a system of weights and measures where each unit is 10 times larger or 10 times smaller than the unit next to it in size. It is sometimes called a decimal system. The Latin word decem means ten.

ohm (say: *OME*)   a unit of electrical resistance.

pace   an old Roman measure of length. The unit of measurement was the distance from the heel of one foot to the heel of the same foot when it next touched the ground, or about five of our feet.

radius   the distance from a point on a circle to the center of the circle, or one-half the diameter.

scruple   a unit of weight in apothecaries' weights equal to 20 grains.

sextant   an instrument used for measuring distances by means of estimating angles.

sterling silver   a fineness of a silver alloy when the amount of silver is 92½ parts silver out of every 100 parts.

tachometer (say: *tuh-KAHM-uh-tr*)   an instrument that measures an engine's revolutions per minute.

time zones   zones set up to help us keep proper time. The Number One Zone runs along the zero meridian. Greenwich, England, is on that meridian. The first zone east of Greenwich keeps its clocks one hour later than Greenwich Standard Time. The first zone west of Greenwich keeps its clocks one hour earlier than Greenwich Standard Time. There are four time zones that run through the United States. They are the Eastern, Central, Mountain, and Pacific Standard Time Zones. When it is 2 P.M. in a city in the Eastern Time Zone, it is 1 P.M. in a city in the Central Time Zone.

tire gauge (say: *GAYGE*)   a gauge for measuring the air pressure in a tire.

troy   a system of weights for measuring the weights of precious stones, precious metals, and drugs. In the troy system, there are 12 ounces to the pound.

type measure   a system for measuring the sizes of type. A point is a unit measuring about 1/72 of an inch. Twelve points, or nearly 1/6 of an inch, forms a unit called a *pica* (say: *PIE-kuh*).

Volta (say: *VAHL-tah*) **Alessandro**   a famous Italian physicist. He did much work in the field of electricity. The volt (rhymes with *colt*), a unit of electrical force, received its name from Volta.

voltmeter (say: *VOLT-me-tr*)   an instrument for measuring electrical force.

watt   a unit of electrical power, named after James Watt, a Scottish inventor, who made the world's first widely-used steam engine.

weather map   a map of our country showing much about air pressure, temperature, and direction of movement of air masses.

INDEX

71